AFRICA

A TRUE BOOK

by
David Petersen

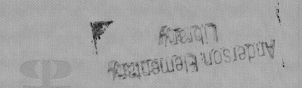

Children's Press®

A Division of Grolier Publishing

New York London Hong Kong Sydney
Danbury, Connecticut

Silverback mountain
gorillas in Rwanda

Reading Consultant
Linda Cornwell
Learning Resource Consultant
Indiana Department of
Education

Visit Children's Press on the Internet at:
http://publishing.grolier.com

Library of Congress Cataloging-in-Publication Data

Petersen, David, 1946–
   Africa / by David Petersen.
      p.   cm. — (A True book)
   Includes bibliographical references and index.
   Summary: A brief overview of the geography, wildlife, history, and
people of Africa.
   ISBN 0–516–20767–9 (lib. bdg.)   0-516-26369-2 (pbk.)
   1. Africa—Juvenile literature. [1. Africa.] I. Title. II. Series.
DT3.P47 1998
960—dc21   97–29745
                                                            CIP
                                                            AC

Contents

Africa is home to people of many different cultures, races, and religions.

A Land of Contrasts

Africa is a land of contrasts. This huge continent features lush tropical rain forests, huge deserts, and vast, grass-covered plains. You can find large, bustling cities and remote wildernesses filled with animals. In some parts of the dry, hot deserts, practically nothing at all lives.

Cairo, Egypt, is the largest of Africa's many bustling cities.

Africa is home to people of many different backgrounds. About one-third of Africa's people live in modern cities. But most Africans make their homes in rural areas and live and dress much like their ancestors. The variety of Africa's people, animals, and land-scapes makes it one of the most fascinating continents on Earth.

Geography

High on Africa's east coast, a point of land juts into the Indian Ocean like a horn. This area includes the nations of Ethiopia and Somalia and is called the Horn of Africa.

Lake Victoria lies just south of the Horn. It is the largest lake in Africa and the source

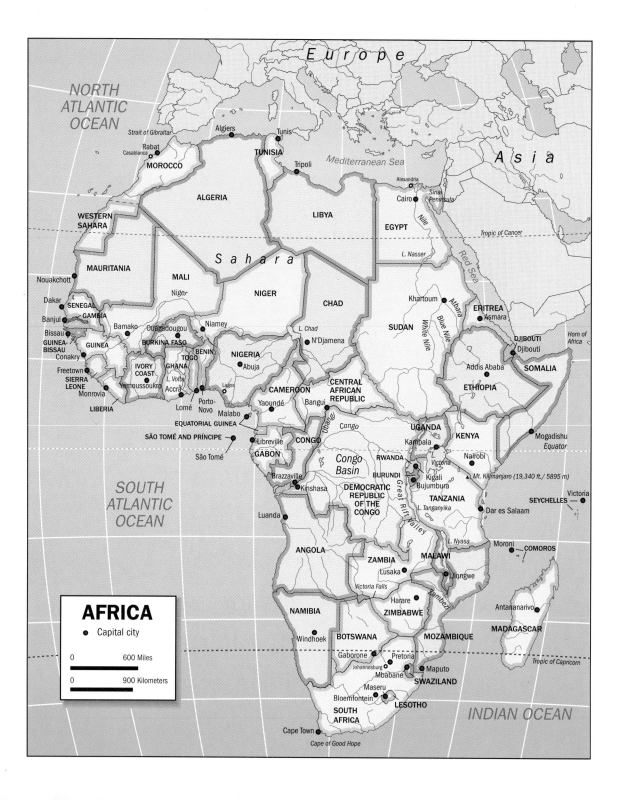

The Nile is the world's longest river.

of the world's longest river, the Nile. Between Lake Victoria and the east coast of Africa rises massive Mount Kilimanjaro. At 19,340 feet (5,895 meters) above the nearby sea, this snow-covered

9

Mount Kilimanjaro (above) is Africa's highest mountain. People from all around Africa and the world come to see beautiful Victoria Falls (right).

peak is Africa's highest point. Madagascar, the world's fourth-largest island, lies 240 miles (386 kilometers) off the east coast of Africa.

Directly below Lake Victoria, like a line of big blue tears, stretches the lake-filled Great Rift Valley. This great canyon system, hundreds of miles long, is visible from the moon. Another famous African land-mark is Victoria Falls, located between Zambia and Zim-babwe in south-central Africa.

Here the waters of the Zambezi River plunge 355 feet (108 m) with a thundering roar.

Africa is the second-largest of Earth's seven continents. Asia, the largest continent, joins Africa at the Sinai Peninsula.

Africa almost touches the continent of Europe to the northwest. The two are separated only by a narrow ocean channel, called the Strait of Gibraltar.

Sahara

Some people think that Africa is all jungle. Actually, only about one-fifth of the continent is forested, and even less is tropical rain forest or jungle. About two-fifths of the continent is covered in open, brushy plains called savanna. The rest is hot, rocky desert.

These mountains of sand in the Sahara are called dunes.

The African Sahara is the world's largest desert. (Sahara is an Arabic word meaning "desert," so if you say "Sahara Desert," you're repeating yourself.) The Sahara covers almost the entire top of the African continent. The hottest temperature ever recorded on Earth was a sizzling 136.4 degrees Fahrenheit (58° Celsius) in Libya, in the Sahara in 1922.

Because the Sahara is so hot and dry, life there can be very hard. Although it is almost as big as the United States, the Sahara supports only about two million people. The United States, by comparison, has

This desert town is built around an oasis. An oasis is an isolated area where water can be found beneath the dry desert ground.

more than a hundred times as many people!

Below the Sahara lies the Congo Basin. Here the land is green and hilly. Because the Congo Basin gets lots of rain, it's crisscrossed with rivers and tangled in tropical rain forests.

Most of the rest of Africa is savanna, open plains covered with grasses, thorny brush, and scattered trees. Across these vast areas roam the largest numbers of wild animals on Earth.

Two-fifths of Africa is covered with grassy plains called savannas.

A View from High Above the Earth

The yellow-brown sands of the Sahara cover almost the entire top of Africa.

Deep green rain forests cover the Congo Basin.

Many lakes stretch across the Great Rift Valley.

Lake Victoria

A Wildlife Wonderland

The different regions of Africa are home to very different kinds of animals.

In the hot, dry deserts, camels have developed the ability to go for long periods without water. Meanwhile, Africa's forests and jungles are alive with tree-loving animals

Because camels (above) can go many days without water, people have used them for centuries to cross the deserts of Africa. Chimpanzees (left) and crocodiles (below) are some of the many animals that live in Africa's forests and rivers.

such as apes, monkeys, birds, and insects. Africa's many lakes, swamps, and rivers are home to huge crocodiles, giant hippos, fish, and long-legged wading birds.

But Africa's greatest wealth of wildlife occupies the savanna and brushlands. Huge herds of zebras, buffaloes, giraffes, rhinos, and antelopes live on these grassy plains. Large carnivores such as lions, leopards, cheetahs, and

The savanna is home to huge herds of animals, including giraffes, zebras, and gnus (above) and the huge white rhinoceros (left).

hyenas follow and hunt the grazing herds.

In many parts of Africa, elephants still roam free. As adults, they are too big and powerful to fear any enemy except humans. Tragically, elephants are often killed illegally for their valuable ivory tusks.

The African elephant is the largest animal on land.

However, ivory poaching is only one of the ways people destroy Africa's wild lands. Every day, in order to survive, Africans cut down trees in the forests and jungles, plow up savannas, and otherwise take over wild areas for human uses.

Of course, people need a place to live and food to eat. But so do wild creatures, and they are entirely at our mercy.

The Big Cats

The African savanna is home to many fierce hunters, including the big cats. The most famous African cats are the lion, the leopard, and the cheetah. Lions live in groups called prides. Leopards prefer to live alone. They are often seen lying in trees. Cheetahs are the fastest animals on land. They can run at speeds up to 70 miles per hour (113 km per hour)!

cheetah

leopard

pride of lions

Motherland

Africa is often called the "Motherland." And rightly so. Scientists believe that Africa was the birthplace of humanity. There, millions of years ago, our earliest ancestors learned to walk upright and began to make and use tools. Human intelligence,

The great pyramids were built by the ancient Egyptians more than four thousand years ago. Ancient Egypt is Africa's oldest civilization

language, and society all evolved in Africa.

And it was from Africa, about a million years ago,

that humans set out on their slow migrations to other continents.

Today, Africa is divided into 53 independent nations. Together, these countries are home to about 732 million people. Black Africans are Africa's first and most numerous people. Black Africans far outnumber all other African races combined. Representing some 800 ethnic groups, black African culture is varied and

Black Africans are the continent's first and most numerous people (above). Many Africans still wear traditional African clothing (left).

rich. Black African art, music, and food have become popular the world over.

Most of the people in northern Africa are Arabs. These Arabic people live in Egypt.

Most of the people in northern Africa are Arabs. Berbers, Asians, and Europeans also make up an important part of Africa's population.

A World of Culture

These men are playing a stringed instrument called a kora at a festival in Dakar, Senegal.

African music, art, dance, and food have become popular all over the world. In fact, many art forms in other countries are influenced by African culture. For example, the rock music popular in the United States takes many of its roots from African music.

A woman in Mali prepares food.

An African drum

Europeans in Africa

Africa was the last of Earth's inhabited continents to be explored by European powers.

A major barrier to early exploration was Africa's unfriendly sea coasts. Arriving ships found high cliffs and few natural ports, making it diffi-cult to land. And once ashore,

Africa's rocky
sea coast was
a barrier to
Europeans
wishing to
explore the
continent.

the rugged terrain, fast rivers,
and dangerous animals dis-
couraged exploration and
settlement.

Even so, more and more Europeans explored and settled in Africa. Exploration of the African interior began in the late 1700s, and by the early 1900s, almost all of Africa was under European control. Belgium, Britain, France, Germany, Holland (the Netherlands), Italy, and Portugal each ruled parts of Africa.

All these foreign powers came to Africa seeking wealth

for themselves. Farming, hunting, and trade in Africa were sources of money. And the world's richest supply of gold and diamonds lay hidden in African soil.

But the earliest source of wealth taken from Africa by foreign powers was human labor. For centuries, black Africans by the thousands were kidnapped and sold into slavery.

Today, those years of slavery and European control are

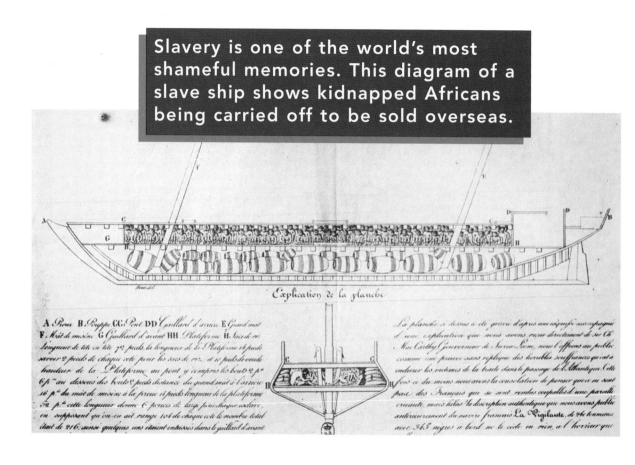

Slavery is one of the world's most shameful memories. This diagram of a slave ship shows kidnapped Africans being carried off to be sold overseas.

looked upon as a tragic time in African history, and little remains of them but their shameful memories. But, even in our lifetime, a remnant of

Africa's darkest days continued in parts of Africa.

For decades in the Republic of South Africa, a small group of white people brutally discriminated against a huge black population. White people went to the best schools and were given good jobs, voting rights, and many other privileges. Black people went to poor schools and were denied civil rights, good jobs, and medical care.

Nelson Mandela (center) greets a crowd of supporters after being elected president of South Africa.

After years of protest within Africa—and pressure from nations around the world— voting rights were finally extended to South African blacks in the 1990s. In 1994, a free government was elected. Nelson Mandela, a black man who had spent many years in jail for speaking out against the unfair laws, was elected president of the new government.

Schools in South Africa are now open to people of all races.

Africa Today... and Tomorrow

Many challenges continue to face Africans of every color and race. Among Africa's problems are illiteracy, unemployment, poverty, disease, starvation, a short life expectancy, crime, war, and overpopulation.

Overpopulation, disease, and poverty still affect many parts of Africa.

The people of Africa are working hard to fix these problems. New schools and hospitals are being built. Education

Education is improving in many of Africa's schools (left). Life is easier in many parts of Africa (right), and the future is bright.

and health care are slowly improving. In many parts of Africa, living and raising a family is becoming easier.

Entering a brand-new century, Africa sees a bright future.

Africa Fast Facts

Area 11,798,000 square miles (30,556,800 square km), including the island of Madagascar

Highest point Mount Kilimanjaro, Tanzania: 19,340 feet (5,895 m) above sea level

Lowest point Lake Assal, Djibouti: 509 feet (155 m) below sea level

Longest river Nile: 4,145 miles (6,670 km) from its headwaters at Lake Victoria (east-central Africa) to the Mediterranean Sea (North Africa)

Number of independent nations 53

Population 732,000,000

To Find Out More

Here are some additional resources to help you learn more about the continent of Africa:

 **Books**

Arnold, Caroline. **African Animals,** Morrow, 1997.

Dell, Pamela. **Nelson Mandela: Freedom for South Africa,** Children's Press, 1994.

Halliburton, Warren J. **Nomads of the Sahara,** Macmillan, 1992.

Halliburton, Warren J. **African Industries,** Silver Burdett, 1993.

Halliburton, Warren J. **African Landscapes,** Silver Burdett, 1993.

Halliburton, Warren J. **Celebrations of African Heritage,** Silver Burdett, 1993.

Silver, Donald M. **African Savanna,** W. H. Freeman, 1995.

Waterlow, Julia. **The Nile,** Raintree Steck-Vaughn, 1993.

Organizations and Online Sites

Africa: Country-Specific Pages
http://www.sas.upenn.edu/ African_Studies/Home_Page/ Country.html

Features country-by-country facts about African nations.

Africa South of the Sahara: Selected Internet Resources
http://www-sul.stanford. edu/depts/ssrg/africa/guide. html

A directory of links to sites about southern Africa. Listed by topic and region.

INTELLiCast: Africa Weather
http://www.intellicast.com/ weather/africa/

Forecasts and weather information for Africa.

Kilimanjaro Climb for CARE
http://outside.starwave.com/ places/africa/index.html

A day-by-day account of an expedition to the top of Kilimanjaro.

The Mandela Page
http://www.anc.org.za/ people/nrmpage.html

Contains information about Nelson Mandela, including a detailed biography.

National Parks and Tourism in Zimbabwe
http://www.mediazw.com/ natparks/index.html

Pictures and information about National Parks and places of interest in Zimbabwe, including Victoria Falls.

Important Words

carnivore an animal that hunts and eats other animals

continent one of seven large land masses of the earth.

discriminate to treat people unfairly because of prejudice

equator an imaginary line drawn around Earth's middle, halfway between the North and South poles

migration a move from one region to another

plain a large, flat area of land

poacher one who kills or steals protected animals or plants

tropical coming from or being in the hot, rainy area near the equator, an imaginary line drawn around the earth's middle

Index

Meet the Author

David Petersen lives with one small wife (Carolyn) and two large dogs (Otis and Angel) in a little cabin on a big mountain in Colorado. He enjoys reading, writing, and the outdoors. His most recent "grown-up" book is *Ghost Grizzlies: Does the Great Bear Still Haunt Colorado?* (Henry Holt & Co.). Mr. Petersen has written many other books on geography for Children's Press, including True Books on all the continents.